EXTREME PLACES

THE MOST REMOTE HOMES ON EARTH

GILES LAROCHE

CLARION
BOOKS
An Imprint of HarperCollinsPublishers

To those who live in these remote locations –G.L.

HarperCollins Children's Books, a division of HarperCollins Publishers,
195 Broadway, New York, NY 10007

HarperCollins Publishers, Macken House,
39/40 Mayor Street Upper, Dublin 1, D01 C9W8, Ireland

Clarion Books is an imprint of HarperCollins Publishers.

Extreme Places: The Most Remote Homes on Earth

harpercollins.com

Library of Congress Control Number: 2022947983
ISBN 978-0-35-869018-4

The artist used a variety of hand-painted papers to create the cut-paper relief illustrations for this book.
Typography by Cara Llewellyn
25 26 27 28 29 RTLO
10 9 8 7 6 5 4 3 2 1

First Edition

INTRODUCTION

Would you be lonely living high on a steep mountainside that becomes snowbound and cut off from the rest of the world in winter? Or bored in a tiny village on an isolated island thousands of miles from any continent? Could you find your way home through the dense jungle of a humid rainforest? Or make your way through a fierce, blinding sandstorm in a scorching hot desert?

Our planet has many places where everyday life appears to be a constant or difficult challenge, whether from isolation, severe climate, or potential harm caused by Earth itself, such as volcanic eruptions or earthquakes—or so it seems to those who do not live there. Yet in many such remote places families learn how to band together and rely on each other, and this spirit of teamwork helps to sustain extreme living. Although there are many survival skills required to adapt to harsh conditions, local people in these communities cherish their desert, polar, mountaintop, or rainforest homes. As one old man in the Spiti Valley in the Himalayas says when the road to his remote village is impassable, "It's too beautiful to leave here anyway."

TRISTAN DA CUNHA

What would it be like to live in the middle of an ocean on a tiny volcanic island that is the most remote spot on Earth? Here you would share your small settlement huddled beneath a volcano with ocean-loving birds such as albatrosses, penguins, and petrels. The only town on the island includes a school, church, and health clinic. Crops of potatoes and pumpkins are grown on the flanks of this mountain, and you can explore the cones of extinct volcanoes, or you could help herd your family's sheep and learn how to shear their wool before painting their skin your favorite color—a local custom.

LOCATION: Some three million years ago a South Atlantic volcano began erupting two miles below sea level. Over time the eruptions created this mountain island halfway between Argentina and South Africa. Because Tristan's terrain is too steep for an airport, all visitors and supplies arrive after a six-day ocean voyage from Cape Town, South Africa, and are ferried ashore in smaller boats—if the stormy seas allow!

WHO LIVES HERE? Tristão da Cunha, a Portuguese explorer, first saw this mountain peak rising abruptly above the sea in 1506 and gave it his name. But the rough surf prevented his landing. The island wasn't permanently settled by the English until 1816, and today it is a British overseas territory where 260 descendants live in the only town: Edinburgh of the Seven Seas. Children, who share only nine common last names, attend school here until age twelve and can further their studies in England or South Africa.

FASCINATING FACT: In 1961, the 6,725-foot-high Queen Mary's Peak suddenly erupted, creating lava flows that forced the relocation of all Tristanians to the United Kingdom. Two years later the eruptions subsided and nearly all returned to resume living in their close-knit and beloved community.

ADAPTING TO EXTREMES: To withstand the strong Atlantic winds, Tristanians' uniquely designed houses have wide gable ends made of heavy volcanic stone. Families grow their own vegetables and raise their own livestock. They trap crawfish—a delicacy called Tristan lobster—from their handcrafted boats and catch yellowtail mackerel and octopus, which is served with teddy cakes—a kind of potato pancake. Playing soccer is a popular after-school activity, and friends gather in the evenings to sing songs about their island, including "The Volcano's Black" and "The Molly," a song about an albatross that lives on the island's cliffs.

SAHARA DESERT

Would you enjoy living in a land of endless windswept sand dunes and mountains? Your family would ride on camels through the hot desert to find new grazing grounds for your sheep and goats and stop at water sources called oases to quench your thirst and rest in the welcome shade of date palm trees. Here you would feed your camels, help set up small solar panels for light, and erect tents to camp in at night when the temperature drops sharply.

LOCATION: The Sahara is a vast desert region in northern Africa about the size of the USA and still expanding in area. It stretches through thirteen countries, from Egypt and Eritrea on the Red Sea of the Indian Ocean to Morocco and Mauritania on the Atlantic.

WHO LIVES HERE? Hardy desert nomads including the Tuaregs ride on the fat-filled humps of their camels across the desert while herding livestock from oasis to oasis. The Moors live in the arid mountains and harvest olives, almonds, and dates, and make cheese from the milk of their camels.

FASCINATING FACT: Millions of years ago, long before humans arrived, this region was dotted with lakes and covered in green until climatic changes gradually caused it to become the Sahara, which means "desert" in Arabic.

ADAPTING TO EXTREMES: In a land of scorching temperatures, scant rainfall, and blinding sandstorms that make breathing difficult and can even bury entire towns, the survival of plants and animals is nearly impossible. But humans have adapted, settling in the mountains where there are streams, or near seasonal oases where dates can always be found and sometimes other crops such as watermelons, beans, and oranges can grow. Meat, vegetables, and a grain called couscous are cooked in small clay tagines. Oasis festivals are popular and feature horse races, rabbit chases, and outdoor markets where the bounty of dates are prepared and enjoyed in a variety of ways. To stay cool, and for protection from the sandy winds, desert dwellers wear long, loose layers of cotton forming a robe called a boubou and cover their heads with turbans or veils.

MENTAWAI ISLANDS

Can you imagine awakening every morning to the musical whoops of bilous frolicking in the rainforest canopy above your head? These primates are rarely seen since they almost never descend to the forest floor. They have such beautiful calls, many islanders believe the bilous have protective jungle spirits guarding over their well-being. If you lived here, you could use your jungle knowledge to show rainforest ecologists animals like scops owls, mouse deer, pig-tailed langurs, leaf-nosed bats, and Siberut macaques. Ecologists study these animals and rare plants, birds, and insects to help preserve and protect their fragile rainforest habitat.

LOCATION: Halfway between the north and south poles, along the Earth's equator, are the Mentawai Islands, an emerald-green chain of some seventy islands of the Indian Ocean lying ninety miles off the coast of West Sumatra, a province of Indonesia. Covered by dense rainforest jungle and prone to frequent earthquakes and tsunamis, which flood the low-lying villages, these isolated islands remain a world of their own.

WHO LIVES HERE? The Mentawai, sometimes called the flower people, are descendants of the ancient tribal inhabitants of Indonesia who first settled these islands around 2000 BCE and remained mostly unaware of other cultures until the mid-twentieth century.

FASCINATING FACT: Some Mentawai decorate their bodies with tattoos to assure recognition by their jungle ancestors in the afterlife. Because these guardian human spirits reside in the rainforest, Mentawai have a profound respect for their environment and especially other living creatures, whom they regard as their neighbors.

ADAPTING TO EXTREMES: Many Mentawai live in stilted communal longhouses called umas or smaller one-story laleps. Both are built using wood planks, bamboo, and grass, which keep their homes cool in the humid jungle. Paddling rivers in dugout canoes, they fish and net shellfish for meals, which can also include chicken, pork, bananas, and sago, a type of starch made from the pith of palm stems. Because mainland Sumatra is just a six-hour ferry ride away from the largest Mentawai island, Siberut, modern technology and communication, such as cell phones and the internet, are constantly challenging many age-old traditions.

VERKHOYANSK

How would you keep your home warm where the ground is permanently frozen? From November to April, the temperature in this tiny village in Siberia remains below freezing, and it is often so cold that being outdoors more than fifteen minutes causes frostbite. Roadside wood fires are always kept burning so you can warm up when walking to a friend's house. You bundle up in an extra warm homemade fur coat and pelt boots to go for reindeer sleigh rides across frozen rivers and into the boreal forests. When the temperature drops to about –70°F, you can hear your breath make sounds the Siberians call "the whisper of angels." In summer, if you stay up late, you can ride a Yakut horse and witness the fabled "white nights," when at midnight the sun dips near the horizon but never sets.

LOCATION: Verkhoyansk is in the district of the Russian Sakha Republic in the northern region called Siberia, which means "the sleeping land." Situated well above the Arctic Circle, it is the coldest settlement on Earth.

WHO LIVES HERE? Descendants of the Cossacks, early inhabitants of central Russia who first settled Verkhoyansk in 1638, live here. Today's population of about 1,300 is half of what it was fifteen years ago. Residents work in nearby tin and gold mines, while others raise cattle, reindeer, hare, and Yakut horses whose extra dense fur keeps them warm.

FASCINATING FACT: On February 7 and 9, 1892, the temperature in Verkhoyansk dropped to –90°F, but on June 20, 2020, it soared to over 100°F, giving the town the record for both coldest and hottest temperatures within the Arctic Circle!

ADAPTING TO EXTREMES: To prepare for the very long, dark Siberian winter, villagers stack blocks of ice outside houses, which they melt for clean drinking and cooking water. Fish, hare, and venison are stored for food in rooms that serve as freezers. Clothes and shoes made locally from fur, pelts, and reindeer hide are the best garments for this climate, far warmer than machine-made synthetic fabrics. Reindeer are trained to pull wooden sleds filled with firewood for heating rooms that are used for sleeping and living.

ISLA NAVARINO

While Verkhoyansk enjoys summer's midnight sun, days on the opposite side of the globe are dark and wintry. Called "the end of the world," Isla Navarino is on one of Earth's most treacherous channels, where the Atlantic and Pacific merge in a turmoil of roiling waters and blustery winds. Growing up here, you would learn how to trap giant king crabs from your family's fishing boat, know where to spot swimming whales, penguins, and seals in the waters below the jagged snowcapped mountains aptly named "the teeth of Navarino," and become familiar with scientists who use the isla as a departure point for expeditions to adjacent Antarctica.

LOCATION: Isla Navarino, Chile, is at the tip of South America and is part of a group of islands called Tierra del Fuego. This archipelago is situated on the Strait of Magellan, named after Portuguese explorer Ferdinand Magellan, who sailed through the only sea route connecting the hemispheres in 1520 on the first recorded circumnavigation of the globe. Its two hamlets, Puerto Toro, founded in 1892 as a fishing port, and Puerto Williams, founded in 1953 as a naval base, are the world's southernmost towns.

WHO LIVES HERE? Puerto Williams' three thousand inhabitants are called Fuegians, or people of the archipelago. They are descendants of the Yaghans and Onas, indigenous people who migrated to Navarino more than ten thousand years ago, and the Spanish who conquered what is now Chile five hundred years ago.

FASCINATING FACTS: The opening of the Panama Canal in 1914 made the long below-the-equator detour through the Strait of Magellan unnecessary. Until then, sailors making their way through the perilous strait depended on bonfires in the settlements they passed to help them navigate, which is the origin of the name Tierra del Fuego or "Land of Fire." These fires kept the Yaghans and Onas warm and provided much-needed safety beacons for ships.

ADAPTING TO EXTREMES: The southern king crab, caught by net from fishing boats, is sold worldwide and provides both food and livelihood for the Fuegians. Antarctic tourism and research facilities also contribute to the economy. Fuegians knit sweaters made from the wool of Patagonian sheep for warmth and protection in the tundra-like climate, which has winds so persistent and harsh, the growth of trees is stunted.

SPITI VALLEY

High above the clouds, in this land of the sky, is a bowl-shaped valley at almost three miles above sea level. It is surrounded by the snow-clad peaks of Earth's highest mountain range, the Himalayas. Here, in the village of Hikkim, you could send letters from the world's highest post office or attend Earth's very highest high school.

Unlike visitors from lower altitudes, who need rest to adjust to the lower oxygen level, you would have no trouble scrambling up the steep, rocky hillsides to herd your family's sheep, yaks, and horses, or to tend your vegetable garden.

LOCATION: The Spiti Valley, which means "the middle land" in Tibetan, is in the state of Himachal Pradesh, India, nestled in the slopes of the Himalayas near the border with Tibet. The only way to reach the more than two hundred villages in the valley is by a narrow, winding, and often impassable road from the market town Kaza three thousand feet below.

WHO LIVES HERE? Spiti families are descendants of Buddhist Indians and Tibetans who arrived in the seventh century. Each village has a monastery where Buddhist monks live. Several of the monasteries are among the world's oldest as well as highest. In spring, Gaddi sheep herders, nomads from the lower elevations, arrive in the valley with their flocks and remain until the snows of late autumn.

FASCINATING FACT: Numerous fossils of sea creatures can be found here, proving the Himalayas are an uplifted ocean bed formed into mountains when the tectonic plates of two continents were joined many millions of years ago.

ADAPTING TO EXTREMES: Deliveries of basic food and medical supplies are unpredictable because the road in and out is often treacherous, either disappearing under snow or blocked by landslides. Spiti Valley people have therefore learned to adapt and live independently, sharing their valley's bounty. They grow beans, barley, peas, and green vegetables; raise livestock; and weave blankets, jackets, and shawls from the wool of their sheep to wear or to trade in outdoor seasonal markets. Thick mud walls and a roof made of timbers covered in mud and thatch keep Spiti's houses cool in summer and warm in winter. Snow is loved here for the spring mountain snowmelt, which flows down the mountainside in channels called kuls to be stored and used in the dry summers when water is scarce.

GÖREME

Is it possible to live inside a mountain? If you lived here, your town would not only have dwellings for people, but animal shelters, churches, and even a hotel hewn out of hills of solidified volcanic ash called tuff. Your home would have rock walls, sandy floors, and tiny windows overlooking an astonishing landscape of eroded rock formations referred to as fairy castles and chimneys.

To get home you'd have to climb steep winding paths. You and your friends could explore caves and hidden underground villages that have been around since ancient times. When the winds and weather are right, you could ascend in the basket of a colorful hot-air balloon to view your fairy castles and cave doorways from high above.

LOCATION: Göreme is one of several settlements in Cappadocia, a region of central Anatolia in present-day Turkey. In ancient times, it was a junction on a storied trade route called the Silk Road that extended thousands of miles from Europe to eastern China.

WHO LIVES HERE? Hittites were the first group to carve out these tuff shelters around 1200 BCE. Göreme has since been inhabited over centuries by several groups of people, including Christian settlers who extended the caves into underground villages to hide from Roman invasions. Today many of the two thousand Turks living in Göreme still inhabit the old cave dwellings.

FASCINATING FACT: In Turkish, Göreme means "one cannot see into here," as caves are a good hiding place, and some say Cappadocia means "the land down below"!

ADAPTING TO EXTREMES: These cave dwellings are prone to damage from erosion and earthquakes, and Cappadocians have added wooden structural columns to make the dwellings safer. The encompassing tuff provides a natural insulation, keeping rooms cool in summer and warm in winter. Stone sofas are carved below windows, creating sunlit places to sit, and kitchens are the highest room so that the stove's hot air can be vented through chimneys to the sky above. In good weather, families grill shish kebabs outside, which they enjoy with stuffed grape leaves and baklava.

FLOATING ISLANDS of the UROS

If you lived here, on the highest lake in the world, your home would float on one of many human-made islands that dot its waters. Your entire island village could even be towed by boats to a different part of the lake! You would become an expert boater, rowing your homemade balsa to another island for school, or even to mainland shores where your family might sell handcrafts at markets and greet visitors. Some islands have protective watchtowers that you could climb to view other lake isles and the distant Andes peaks.

LOCATION: More than a hundred miles long, nearly a thousand feet deep, and over twelve thousand feet above sea level, Lake Titicaca lies in a valley in the Andes mountain range of Peru and Bolivia and is home to some sixty floating villages.

WHO LIVES HERE? The Uros, a South American people, built their first floating islands more than five hundred years ago to isolate themselves from Inca empire invasions, and now proclaim the lake as their own. Up to ten families live on an island, and some even have stores, clinics, and small schools. The Uros love to welcome visitors, happily taking them to their floating homes on their beautifully constructed balsas, small boats that can hold up to twenty people.

FASCINATING FACT: The reeds and stems of an aquatic plant called totora are used not just to construct the island, but as a building material for houses, watchtowers, and balsas. Its tender white roots can be eaten, and the flowers can be brewed into a pain-soothing tea.

ADAPTING TO EXTREMES: The Uros rope together four-foot-thick blocks of totora stems to form the floating foundation of the islands, which are then covered with layers of reed mats to make a floor. To prevent their island from drifting away, long, tough totora stems are anchored to the lake bottom. The Uros enjoy fishing from their islands and balsas, catching catfish, trout, and amanto. They have even trained a tethered aquatic bird called a cormorant to catch fish for them! Many families' floating homes have motorized propellers, refrigeration, TVs, and lights run by solar panels—one island broadcasts music from an Uros radio station.

ATAFU ATOLL

Is it possible to live on a speck of an island constructed entirely by tiny sea creatures? Rising barely above sea level in the vast Pacific, atolls are small, often ring-shaped, and composed of coral reefs that surround a quiet lagoon. If you lived there, you would feel as though the ocean was your world, you would learn to swim soon after you learned to walk, and you would become expert at diving, snorkeling, and fishing.

LOCATION: Atafu is one of three atolls in the South Pacific territory of New Zealand called Tokelau. Lying just west of the International Date Line, where one day changes to the next, Atafuans are the last on Earth to see the sunset every day.

WHO LIVES HERE? When it was first visited by a British sailor in 1765, no one lived on Atafu. Years later, a young Polynesian couple and their seven children established the first settlement, coming from Samoa three hundred miles away. Descendants of these seven, known as "the seven houses," gather annually in New Zealand to celebrate their role in Atafu history, and today the more than five hundred inhabitants speak Tokelauan, Samoan, and English.

FASCINATING FACT: While humans construct artificial islands like those on Lake Titicaca, coral atolls are made by thousands of colonies of minuscule polyp-like sea creatures named coelenterates that live within their secreted rocklike enclosures called corals. Over time, these growing coral reefs emerge above sea level, forming a protective barrier from the ocean waves for the tranquil lagoon within.

ADAPTING TO EXTREMES: Freshly picked coconuts, pawpaws, and bananas and freshly caught tuna, shrimp, and crabs are the islanders' favorite foods. Atafuans have devised a unique fishing method called "noose fishing" using knotted ropes. They weave palm fronds into window shades and floor mats. Houses, furniture, and oceangoing boats are made from the durable wood of the tauanave tree, and its large trunks are hollowed out into single-hull dugout canoes for paddling in the lagoon that can easily be carried from home to shore.

GOBI DESERT

If you were a nomad living in this cold, arid desert where patchy grass and rocks seem to stretch to the horizon in all directions, you and your family would herd your cattle, sheep, goats, and yaks from horseback, from camelback, or even by truck to a new location miles away. Here you would reassemble your portable house called a ger. Riding a horse bareback (without a saddle) might be tricky and uncomfortable at first, but learning how to ride a camel requires special skills. Unlike horses, camels can kneel to the ground, making it easier to mount their backs to sit between their two humps.

LOCATION: Gobi means "waterless" in Mongolian, and this vast desert, twice the size of Texas, lies in northwest China and southern Mongolia between the Altai and Bei mountain ranges.

WHO LIVES HERE? Although Mongols and Han Chinese have shared this land for over a hundred thousand years, harsh living conditions limit permanent human settlements. Most inhabitants live as nomads, seeking out fresh pastures for their livestock. They visit soums, small village-like centers where there are schools, clinics, and markets and where homeschooling kits are available for nomadic children.

FASCINATING FACT: Landlocked Mongolia is one of the world's most sparsely populated areas. Even animals have difficulty adapting to the climate of extreme cold and heat. Wild horses outnumber humans three to one, and two-humped Bactrian camels carry people and goods throughout the Gobi. With luck, a lone snow leopard might be spied bounding away over distant terrain.

ADAPTING TO EXTREMES: First designed by Mongols thousands of years ago, ger means "home" and has become symbolic of life in the Gobi. Supported by wooden poles and covered in felt, these structures are easily taken down, transported, and reassembled after a long day of travel through the desert. Upon erecting their gers, nomads enjoy lamb or goat cooked in a wok, served with rice and yogurt, and steaming hot camel's or mare's milk with sweet cookies as dessert. For protection against the cold and to stay comfortable while riding, Mongols wear a leather hat, boots, and a long robe-like garment called a deel made of wool, cotton, or silk, tied at the waist with a colorful sash.

AOGASHIMA

Would you be afraid to live inside the crater of an active volcano? No eruption has occurred on this island for over two hundred years. But should it happen, you would know the warning signs indicating dangerous movement of molten lava deep within your volcano and have time to safely escape to nearby islands. Instead of fearing it, you would use the steam heat from volcanic vents to cook eggs and sweet potatoes, and relax with your family in the warmth of natural saunas after hiking along the jagged walls encircling the basin-like crater geologists call a caldera.

LOCATION: Two hundred and forty miles south of Tokyo is Aogashima, the southernmost and least populated of Japan's Izu Islands chain, which volcanic activity gradually created over the remains of long extinct undersea calderas. Today the Ikenosawa caldera and its walls form the island's dramatic circular coast. Nestled in the center of this large basin are a village and yet another smaller caldera called Maruyama—this one is still active!

WHO LIVES HERE? We don't know when Aogashima was first settled, but three hundred people were living there when Maruyama last erupted in 1785. Survivors were evacuated and Aogashima remained uninhabited for fifty years. Today it is one of Japan's least populated islands, with only about 170 residents who prefer living apart from the hustle and bustle of the more urban islands.

FASCINATING FACT: Aogashima is just one of over a hundred active volcanoes scattered throughout the Japanese islands. Using land-based instruments and satellite photography, scientists constantly monitor these volcanoes for threatening seismic activity, such as earth movement, to alert local governments and residents.

ADAPTING TO EXTREMES: In contrast to the constant threat of the volcano, the lifestyle of Aogashima's inhabitants emphasizes enjoyment of the natural beauty of the island. Their days are filled with hiking through the lush forest, tending vegetable gardens and fruit tree orchards, and swimming, snorkeling, and sailing in the crystal clear ocean waters. It's little wonder today's residents choose to remain on their peaceful tropical volcano—as long as Maruyama stays asleep!

SOCOTRA

If you lived on this vast, parched island of granite and karst rock formations, you would be familiar with trees and animals not found anywhere else on Earth, including the dragon's blood tree, the oddly shaped cucumber tree, and the golden-winged grosbeak. You and your friends would know where to gather sweet pomegranates for lunch, where to watch the Socotran chameleon change color, and how to avoid the blue baboon tarantula. You could explore hidden stalagmite caves, stroll through meadows of umbrella-shaped trees, and then cool off at a sandy beach while investigating shipwrecks in the company of dolphins.

LOCATION: From space, Socotra looks like a part of the fabled Horn of Africa that has broken away and floated out into the Arabian Sea of the Indian Ocean. It is far closer to Africa than to its home country of Yemen on the Arabian Peninsula three hundred miles to the north.

WHO LIVES HERE? Socotra has only been occupied sporadically since the Paleolithic era. For the last two thousand years it has been inhabited by seafaring people of Indian and Somali origin. Over fifty thousand people live in six hundred tiny villages of stone houses scattered throughout Socotra, the largest being Hadīboh, where there is a harbor and small airport.

FASCINATING FACT: Scientists are challenged by Socotra because of its unusual forms of life. Deriving from its remoteness, ferocious heat, and drought-like conditions, the island is regarded as one of the most isolated, inhospitable places on Earth. Many animal and plant species have evolved here that are endemic, meaning that they live or grow only on Socotra, which is what scientists find so fascinating.

ADAPTING TO EXTREMES: Often called "the alien island" because of the strange flora and exotic landscape, the Socotrans refer to their island as an "abode of bliss." Adept at self-sustainment, the Socotri skillfully manage their fragile land. Families build their own homes using local stone, and with few roads, vehicular traffic is limited. Residents fish and dive for pearls; raise camels, goats, and cattle; grow their own crops; and harvest figs and wild oranges.

ATKA

If you lived in this isolated village in Alaska, you and about a dozen fellow students would use wooden boardwalks over the muddy or snow-covered earth to get to school. On the way, you would see bald eagles soaring overhead, puffins diving, seals and sea lions frolicking in the nearby harbor, and reindeer strolling the streets. The wildlife would seem to be the real inhabitants, and you and your family would feel like guests.

LOCATION: Atka Island, one of the few inhabited islands of sixty-nine in the 1,100-mile-long Aleutian chain, is the westernmost permanent settlement in North America, closer to Hong Kong, China, than to Washington, DC. The Aleutians are often enveloped in dense fog in summer. In winter, snow covers the treeless mountains, making satellite images of the chain of islands look like a long strand of pearls draped across the Bering Sea below Asia and Siberia.

WHO LIVES HERE? Atka is a native word meaning "guardian spirit," and most Atkans are descendants of an indigenous Unangan people who have lived in the Aleutians for thousands of years. In 1741, Russian seal hunters arrived, intruding upon the native culture by building churches and enforcing fishing and hunting employment. Although English is now common, many Atkans still speak their native Aleut language, which is also taught in school in this close-knit community.

FASCINATING FACT: During the ice age ten thousand years ago, when the northern hemisphere was covered with glaciers, the sea level consequently dropped, exposing a continuous land bridge 1,500 miles wide between Siberia and Alaska. Archaeological finds and DNA analysis prove that before the sea level rose again, humans used this bridge to cross over by foot and populate the Americas, which until then had no human presence.

ADAPTING TO EXTREMES: Atkans hunt seals, sea lions, and waterfowl and fish for cod, salmon, and halibut from traditional Aleutian kayaks called baidarkas built from driftwood and sealskin. Today motorized all-terrain vehicles are widely used to get about, and residents are seeking improved electronic communication with mainland Alaska. Atkans cherish their heritage and are highly skilled at carving intricate, artistic designs on reindeer antlers and walrus tusks, which are collected worldwide.

4
13
10
7
6
11
2
12
3
9
1

1) TRISTAN DA CUNHA

2) SAHARA DESERT

3) MENTAWAI ISLANDS

4) VERKHOYANSK

5) ISLA NAVARINO

6) SPITI VALLEY

7) GÖREME

8) FLOATING ISLANDS

9) ATAFU ATOLL

10) GOBI DESERT

11) AOGASHIMA

12) SOCOTRA

13) ATKA

A NOTE ON THE ARTWORK

Each illustration for this book involves many stages of drawing, cutting, and gluing multiple layers of paper on painted backgrounds for every object depicted, whether buildings, boats, people, animals, trees, or whatever. Spacers separate each object to give the illusion of varying depth to the assembled final composition, which is then photographed for publication.

1: Background sketching

2: Painting

3: Element cutting and coloring

4: Careful placement

5: Glue time

6: Final touches!

SELECTED SOURCES

Binwaber, Muneer. *Socotra: Story of the Enchanted Island!* Self-published, CreateSpace, 2014.

Britt-Gallagher, Susan, and Tricia Hayne. *St Helena: Ascension and Tristan da Cunha.* 4th ed. Lanham, MD: The Globe Pequot Press, 2021.

Ceitelis, Jack. *The Chilean Landscape.* Santiago, Chile: Librairie française, 1982.

de Villiers, Marq, and Sheila Hirtle. *Sahara: The Extraordinary History of the World's Largest Desert.* New York: Walker and Company, 2002.

Eliot, Joshua, and Jane Bickersteth. *Sumatra Handbook.* Bath, England: Footprint Handbooks, 2000.

Foster, Sophie. "Tokelau." Encyclopedia Britannica. (www.britannica.com/place/Tokelau/History)

Goltz, Thomas, and Tony Gillotte. *Turkey.* London: Insight Guides, 1988.

Khagta, Himanshu. *Life in Spiti.* India: Blurb Inc., 2017.

Man, John. *Gobi: Tracking the Desert.* New Haven, CT: Yale University Press, 1999.

Nalewicki, Jennifer. "The Sleepy Japanese Town Built Inside an Active Volcano." *Smithsonian*, July 5, 2016.

Oberheu, Susanne, and Michael Waldenpohl. *Cappadocia: A Travel Guide through the Land of Fairy Chimneys and Rock Castles.* Norderstedt, Germany: Books on Demand GmbH, 2010.

Steen, Bill, Athena Steen, and Eiko Komatsu. *Built by Hand: Vernacular Buildings Around the World.* Salt Lake City, UT: Gibbs Smith Publisher, 2003.

Theroux, Marcel. *Visiting Verhoyansk, Siberia.* New York: Travel and Leisure, 2009.

Wehner, Ross, and Renée del Gaudio. *Lake Titicaca.* New York: Avalon Travel, 2011.

Wilson, Kenneth F., and Jeff Richardson. *The Aleutian Islands of Alaska: Living on the Edge.* Fairbanks, Alaska: University of Alaska Press, 2008.